Well Spoke

Gaynor Ramsey
Hilary Rees-Parnall

Longman

Addison Wesley Longman Limited,
Edinburgh Gate, Harlow,
Essex CM20 2JE, England
and Associated Companies throughout the world.

First published 1989
Eleventh impression 1998

Set in 9/11pt Linotron Palatino
Produced through Longman Malaysia, ACM

ISBN 0 582 02090   5

Acknowledgements
The publishers would like to thank all those involved
in advising on this material in its draft stages.

We are grateful to the following for permission to reproduce
copyright material:

Barnaby's Picture Library for pages 10 (right), 20 (top middle
right), 24 (upper middle), 24 (bottom left), 30 (left), 40 (top
right), 40 (dog, horse, stag, rabbit, squirrel, mouse), 48
(left), 48 (middle); Our thanks to British Rail for permission
to use the Senior Citizens Railcard leaflet copy; Camera
Press Ltd for pages 40 (cat, camel), 59 (left); The J Allan Cash
Photolibrary for pages 20 (top right), 21, 40 (fox, duck, goat,
frog) 59 (middle right); Child to Child for page 27; Daily
Mirror/Syndication International Ltd for page 22 (bottom);
Roger Goffe for page 15; Photo Sally & Richard Greenhill for
pages 10 (left), 20 (top left), 20 (top middle left); Guinness
Brewing for page 54 (top); Willis Hall for page 28 (left);
International Management Group (UK) Inc. for page 12;
K-Shoemakers Ltd for page 16 (right); Map courtesy of
Kuoni Travel Ltd for page 18 (top left); McGill & Poelsma/
Reproduced by permission of The Evening Standard for
pages 37, 55; The National Society for the Prevention of
Cruelty to Children for page 27 (top right); Network
Photographers for pages 30 (right), 48 (right); Popperfoto for
page 30 (middle); Rex Features Ltd for page 28 (middle left),
28 (middle right), 28 (right); Save The Children Fund for
page 27 (top middle); Sheraton Hotels/WCRS Mathews
Marcantonio for page 16 (top); Spar (UK) Ltd for page 16
(left); Frank Spooner Pictures for page 11; Sunshine Fund for
Blind Babies & Young People for page 27 (left); UNICEF for
page 27 (bottom right); Elizabeth Whiting & Associates for
page 25; Courtesy of Woman's Own for page 13; World
Society for the Protection of Animals for page 40 (top left).

We are grateful to the following for permission to reproduce
copyright material:

Bales Tours Ltd for an extract from *Bales Worldwide Brochure*
1988/9; Century Hutchinson Publishing Group Ltd for
simplified extract 'I've seen a Ghost' by Jon Pertwee from
True Stories from Show-Business ed. Richard Davis; Kuoni
Travel Ltd for an extract from the *Kuoni Worldwide Brochure*
1987–8; the Author, Christopher Logue for his poem
'London Airport' from *Ode to the Dodo* pubd. Jonathan Cape
Ltd; The Observer Ltd for article from 'Pendennis Page' in
Observer Colour Magazine 31.5.87; SOLO Syndication &
Literary Agency for simplified extracts from article by Willis
Newlands in *Daily Mail* 22.2.88 (c) Daily Mail & *Guinness
Book of Records* 1988 (c) Guinness Book of Records; The
Southern Publishing Company (Westminster Press Ltd) for
article 'Helping addicts keep a balance' by Jeannine
Williamson in *EVENING ARGUS, BRIGHTON* 5.4.88; Jane
Asher, Rosie Barnes, Willis Hall & Marsha Hunt for
simplified extracts from interviews in the article 'When Was
It For You?' in *Sunday Times Magazine* 15.11.87; Syndication
International for extracts 'Alex, Anna, Martin, Peter,
Harriet, Fionia' from *Woman's Own* 13.2.88.

All photographs not listed above were taken by Longman
Photographic Unit.

Illustrated by Hardlines, Norah Kenna, Frances Lloyd and
Michael Salter.

Contents

Map of the book

Unit	Title	Thematic areas	Assumed language
1	Rural and Urban	Description of transport, atmosphere and leisure time in town and country; influence of surroundings on health – stress; the homeless in cities; village, town and city life	Present simple; *would like; would prefer*
2	Love	Feelings towards people, places and things; children's views on love; descriptions of character; the commercialisation of love	Present simple; past simple
3	Good Luck and Bad Luck	Omens of good and bad luck; ways of wishing people luck	Present simple; *going to*
4	Advertising	Effective advertisements; describing products for advertising purposes; banning advertising	Present simple; *must be; could be;* adjectives
5	Fast and Slow	Expressing speed; forms of transport; holidays and travel; the pace of life	Present simple; *would;* comparatives and superlatives
6	Family Life	Different size families; good and bad things about families; having children; the family and work	Present simple; *would like; should*
7	Telepathy	Sending and receiving messages; Uri Geller's psychic powers; telepathic happenings; attitudes towards telepathy	Present simple; past simple
8	Traditional and Modern	Describing different styles – atmosphere; rooms and furniture; changing tastes	Present simple; *must be; could be; might; would; will be*
9	Childhood	Memories of childhood; habits in childhood; charities working for children; health and illness in childhood	Present simple; past simple; *would; used to*
10	Becoming an Adult	The process of growing up; the landmarks of adulthood, attitudes to adulthood	Present simple; past simple; future simple; *can*
11	Old Age	Describing old people and their lives; predictions about old age; special help for old people; differences in one's life as one gets older	Present simple; *going to;* future simple; past simple
12	Dirt and Rubbish	Describing dirt and cleanliness; tidiness; talking about rubbish	Present simple; *could; wish* + past perfect; adjectives
13	Fears and Phobias	Things people are afraid of; explanation of existing fears; fears for the future	Present simple; past simple; *used to; may; might*

Unit	Title	Thematic areas	Assumed language
14	Women and Men	Children's views on the opposite sex; differences in education, hobbies and expectations for boys and girls; statistical comparison; unusual jobs; attitudes towards one's sex	Present simple; past simple; *would; would like*
15	Strange Stories	Talking about 'records' (e.g. tallest, shortest); ghost stories	Past simple; *must be; can't be; might be/have been; could be/have been;* superlatives
16	Animals	Comparing how people keep animals; different kinds of animals, animals as food, attitudes towards animals	Present simple; present continuous; past simple; *would; should;* passive
17	Festivals and Holidays	Different kinds of festivals and holidays; the pros and cons of holidays; your ideal holiday	Present simple; *would like/love*
18	Pet Hates	Expressing dislike; different kinds of pet hates; curing pet hates	Present simple; past simple; *used to; could*
19	Hot and Cold	Words relating to 'hot' and 'cold'; situations of 'too hot' and 'too cold'; influencing the temperature; climate; fire	Present simple; present perfect; second conditional
20	Addiction	Attitudes of society towards smoking, drinking and drug-taking; effects of these habits; helping people who are addicted; other addictions	Present simple; present continuous; past simple; *may; might;* second conditional; *can't stop* + gerund
21	Noises and Sounds	Sounds heard in various places; pleasant and unpleasant sounds; attitudes towards noise; dealing with disturbing noise; consideration towards other people	Present simple; past simple; present perfect; *would*
22	Work	Working styles in different societies; talking about work; value of a job; attitudes towards work	Present simple; *would; should;* passives; *would like*
23	Optimism and Pessimism	Comparison of optimist's and a pessimist's view; how optimistic or pessimistic we are; 'up' and 'down' moods	Present simple; future simple; present perfect; third conditional; *like* + gerund
24	Anger	Describing anger; proverbs about anger; expressing emotions; giving advice on anger; personal experience	Present simple; past simple; present perfect; second and third conditional; *should*
25	Crime and Punishment	Various types of crime and punishment; analysis of a case; the consequences of a long prison sentence	Past simple; *should have done*
26	Taking Risks	Everyday risks; insurance; professional risk-takers; risk and responsibility	Present simple; second conditional; *might*

To the teacher

The aim of the material in *Well Spoken* is to motivate pre-intermediate learners of English to take part in conversations and discussions of various lengths and levels, about things that are either within their experience or that they can speculate about.

There are twenty-six units in the book, covering a wide range of topics, each of which is looked at from several different angles. The order of the units within the book was decided according to the expected level of learner output. However, the units are completely independent of each other and could be used in any order. The units vary in style from very factual to highly personalised. Whatever the type of unit, learners should always be encouraged to take a personal stand on the topic, rather than treat it as something remote. The choice of topics in *Well Spoken* leaves little opportunity for remoteness and the treatment of the topics demands active and willing participation on the part of the learners and of the teacher.

The long-term aim of *Well Spoken* is to increase learners' fluency level and therefore the teacher should take a secondary role whenever possible. Correction of language should only be done on the spot when it is clear that a serious misunderstanding is taking place. Otherwise, the teacher can note down mistakes to be dealt with later – although this should not be done in a way that either inhibits the learners or prevents the teacher from taking part. Correction purely for the sake of accuracy, which disturbs the flow of an activity, should be avoided.

WHAT SORT OF PREPARATION NEEDS TO BE DONE FOR THESE ACTIVITIES?

The amount of preparation depends mainly on the learners' language level, their familiarity with the necessary vocabulary, their experience of activities which emphasise fluency rather than accuracy, and their willingness and ability to use the language they know spontaneously.

If the teacher realises that some vocabulary necessary for a particular activity is not known, then this should be pre-taught. The technique of letting students ask for vocabulary items they think they'll need is a very useful and productive way of pre-teaching vocabulary for all types of activities.

HOW DO THE LEARNERS ACTUALLY WORK ON THE ACTIVITIES?

Most of the activities can be carried out either in pairs or small groups. This is generally indicated in the instructions or introductions to the activities. Where there is no indication, the teacher can decide how to use the activity – and this will depend greatly on the size of the class. Ideally the teacher should develop a fast and effective way of dividing the class so that students work with different partners and in different groups as often as possible.

WHAT IS IN THE UNITS?

The units do not follow a regular pattern, although there are some characteristics which recur. The table of contents on pages 4–5 shows the topic and the expected language output of each unit. There is no special attention paid to vocabulary content in this table as the range of vocabulary needed and produced will vary greatly from class to class. The activities are introduced in many different ways; from photographs, drawings and authentic texts to vocabulary tasks and questionnaires. Among the activity types that recur are two which always have a title:

Make your teacher talk – where the students are supplied with a few questions to help them do just that!

Class talk – which occurs in every unit, to bring the class together again for a final discussion. There are, nevertheless, separate instructions for each of these Class talk activities as they vary in procedure.

Assuming that there are topics and activities in this book that will interest the learners, there are some other important factors which greatly influence whether or not the material leads to successful classroom interaction. The students

a) should learn to equip themselves for talking about a topic, i.e. request necessary vocabulary and expressions.
b) should be responsible for the carrying out of the activities and tasks.
c) should try to work with everyone in the class and with the teacher on a personal level, and try to develop a genuine interest in everyone present.
d) work with the teacher to create a relaxed atmosphere in the classroom.

If all these recommendations are met then a class stands a very good chance of having a lot of interesting and challenging conversations as part of their English learning experience.

The **Key** at the back of the book provides answers to the activities which are based on specific information. The teacher may want to refer to the key when preparing a unit. In addition, certain exercises in the book suggest that students can check their own answers in the key after completing the activity. It is obviously important to ensure that students complete an activity before checking their answers in the book.

To the student

There are many, many things for you and your fellow students to talk about in *Well Spoken*. Most of the responsibility for making these discussions successful lies with you, and not with your teacher. Try to say as much as you can about the topics, and always try to relate the topics to your own personal experiences and your opinions. You may sometimes feel that there is something very personal that you don't want to say – well, the best thing to do is not to say it. You will soon agree, however, that learning a language is much more interesting if that language is used to talk about meaningful topics in a personal way.

Good luck with *Well Spoken*.

UNIT 1 Rural and Urban

Different lifestyles

1 The comments on the left in the table below could be made by both the man and the woman in the pictures. Work with a partner and make some notes to explain what you think they might mean by these statements.

Public transport is difficult.	*too crowded, rush hour terrible, buses are blocked by cars*	*not enough, two buses a day, bad connections, need car*
It's easy to make friends here.		
Physical exercise is a part of my everyday life.		
The atmosphere of the place is really special.		
I don't have to travel far to find what I want.		
I enjoy going out to the theatre – it's another world.		
There's a good choice of leisure time activities.		
There's always something happening here.		

2 Work in groups of three or four. Choose four of the categories below and make a detailed list of how they may be different in the country and in a city.

In the country

- Your health
- Holidays
- The clothes people wear
- Stress
- The people
- Rainy weather

In a city

Make your teacher talk!

3 Ask your teacher about his/her attitude towards town life and country life. Find out:

a) if he/she grew up in a town or in the country
b) if he/she lives in a town or in the country now
c) where he/she would prefer to live
d) what he/she thinks are the best and worst things about country life
e) what he/she thinks are the best and worst things about city life

A problem to solve

4 One major problem in big cities is housing – some people just don't have anywhere to live. The authorities in San Francisco seem to have an answer.

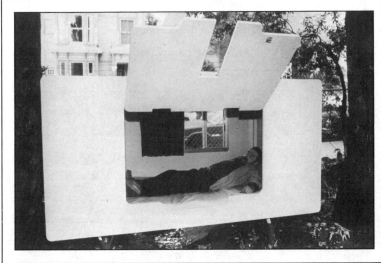

◀ INTERCITY SLEEPER

This must be the first time that a city has decided to send vagrants packing – literally. San Francisco has just authorised the sale of some human suitcases, known as 'City Sleepers'. The hideous-looking cartons measure three metres by one metre and are designed to give vagrants a place to sleep at night. When he reads this, some bright spark at British Telecom is going to work out whether the old red telephone boxes can be turned to this use as well.

What do you think of this solution?
a) Is it practical?
b) Has it got any disadvantages?
c) How do you think you would feel in one of these 'City Sleepers'?
d) Can you think of a better solution for the homeless?

Class talk

5 How do you feel about the place where you live?
- Does it have enough to offer?
- Would you prefer to live somewhere else?
- What are the good things and the bad things about the village, town or city where you live?

Love

Vocabulary

1 Love doesn't only mean romantic love. There are many different kinds of love – different levels of feeling towards people, places and things.

Number these words from 1 to 9 in the order you think is best (1 = positive feelings, 9 = negative feelings).

	be fond of		worship		not like very much
2	adore	4	like	5	love
8	dislike	1	idolise	9	hate

Choose five of these words and tell your partner about people, places or things you know, using those five words.

Talk about your feelings

2 Write your answers in the first two columns below, and then ask your partner about the people, places and things on his/her list and write his/her answers in the second two columns. Tell each other something about the likes and dislikes that you've written down.

What do you love or really like very much?

	I really like (perhaps love) . . .	I'm not very fond of . . .	My partner really likes (perhaps loves). . .	My partner isn't very fond of . . .
a country				
a town				
a type of music, a singer or composer				
a type of film				
something to eat				
something to drink				
a person of the opposite sex				
a person of the same sex				
a child				
an animal				

3 Love is . . .
    . . . sharing an umbrella in a storm.
    . . . giving him your last chocolate.
    . . . telling her she's more beautiful
        than yesterday.
Work in groups of at least four. Think of some more endings for 'Love is . . .' (you needn't be too serious about this!).

_____

_____

_____

love is...

II·21

. . . *washing up together.*

4 Now for a more serious think about partnerships between men and women. Divide your class into a men's group and a women's group. The men's group should make a list of what they think men usually look for or fall for in women, and the women should make a list of what women look for or fall for in men.

Read out your lists to each other and watch the reactions. You can, of course, make any comments you want – in agreement or in disagreement.

5 Here are some English proverbs which have the word 'love' in them. They are general comments on love. Work in groups of three or four to make suggestions about their meanings.
a) One cannot love and be wise.
b) Love is blind.
c) Love me, love my dog.
d) Love will find a way.

What is love?

6 Here are some comments made by young children about love. What experiences or observations do you think are behind these comments?

Fiona, 6
I love my friends because they play with me. I love Mummy. I cuddle her. The bad thing about love is that you always have to get married.

Alex, 6
People who love each other rub noses. I say hello and wave my hand. If I wanted to show a boy I loved him I would give him a game. I'd give a girl a dolly.

Harriet, 5
Love is care. I love my gran and grandad, but older people don't love each other. I've got an older sister but I don't love her because she is always being nasty.

Martin, 6
I love Anna but I haven't told her. And I love my mummy. She shows she loves me by doing things for me, like washing up.

Anna, 6
Love is very nice, it makes me feel happy. I love Ben because he's good looking. I don't think I'll get married. I won't love anyone when I'm older.

Peter, 5
I love Abigail. Sometimes I hug her and kiss her. I've already asked her to marry me and I went down on one knee. I'll marry her when I'm 31.

Class talk

7 Valentine's Day (February 14th) is the day when people traditionally tell others that they love them by sending cards (sometimes anonymously) or by giving flowers or a present.
- What do you think about the way love has become commercialised? Has it become too commercialised?
- Give some examples of how love is exploited in advertising in your country.

Good Luck and Bad Luck

Vocabulary

black cat
number thirteen
opening an umbrella indoors
crossed knives
horseshoe
spilled salt
walking under a ladder
shooting star

1 a) Match these words with the pictures:

i)

ii)

iii)

iv)

v)

vi)

vii)

viii)

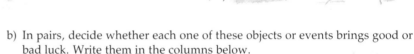

b) In pairs, decide whether each one of these objects or events brings good or bad luck. Write them in the columns below.

GOOD LUCK	BAD LUCK	DON'T KNOW

c) In groups of four, think of some more things which bring good or back luck in your country. Write them in the columns above.

Compare your ideas with another group. Add their ideas to yours.

Do some of the ideas contradict each other? For example, is a black cat lucky for some people and not for others?

Do you know any things from other countries which are supposed to bring good or bad luck?

Bad luck?

2 With your partner, look at this cartoon. Write in the final words.

Talk to the rest of the class and tell them how you have finished the cartoon. Compare all the endings and choose the best one.

Lucky or unlucky?

3 a) What's your lucky colour? _____

What are your lucky clothes? _____

Have you got a lucky charm (a favourite pen, a teddy bear, a ring) which you like to take with you to an exam or job interview? _____

b) Talk to your partner and find out what's lucky for him/her. Write your answers in the chart.

	ME	*MY PARTNER*
lucky colour		
lucky clothes		
lucky charm		

Is there anything you think is unlucky for you? _____

What about your partner? _____

Make your teacher talk!

4 Ask your teacher which things are lucky and unlucky for him/her.

Ask your teacher to explain the expression 'Touch wood!'.

Class talk

5 How would you wish these people good luck? Would you send a card, a letter or a present, or telephone and speak to them? What would you say or write?
- a friend who is going for an interview for a job
- a neighbour who is going to take a driving test
- someone who is going to take an exam
- friends who are going to get married
- a friend who is going to have a baby
- friends who are moving into a new home

Advertising

Talk about advertisements

1 a) Look at this advertisement. What do you think it is for?

Talk to your partner about it. Do you agree with each other? Have you got different ideas? Discuss the reasons for your opinions.

b) Tell the rest of the class what you think. How many different ideas have people thought of? What are the clues people have used?

Ask your teacher to tell you what the advertisement is for. Were you right?

2 Now look at these two advertisements.

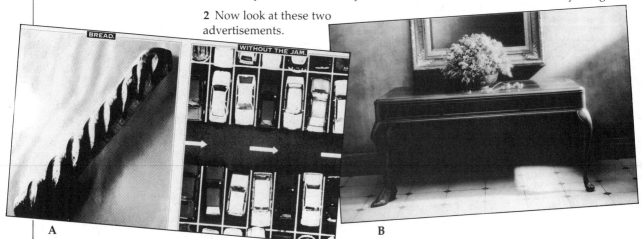

A

B

In groups of three, discuss these questions.
a) What do you think each advertisement is for? What tells you?
b) Is it a good advertisement? Why/Why not?
c)) Would it encourage you to buy the product?

When you have finished your discussion, check with your teacher what each advertisement is for. Were you right?

3 a) Imagine you have the job of selling a new washing powder. Think of at least five adjectives you could use to sell it. Use a dictionary if you want to.
b) Work in a group of four to six people. Tell each other about your words. How many have you got the same? Which ones are the best?
c) Now do the same with a new car.
d) Look at your list of adjectives for washing powder, and your list for a car. Are any of them the same? What qualities have you chosen to emphasise for each one?

Talk about your feelings

4 In Britain, cigarette advertising is banned on television for health reasons. Do you think this is a good idea? Why/Why not?
a) Are there any other products you feel should not be advertised on television? Think about these things for one minute by yourself.

alcohol   children's toys
fast cars   pregnancy testers
contraceptives   medicines

Any others?
b) Work in groups of three. Compare your ideas. Do you agree? Which ones do you disagree about? Discuss your reasons.

Class talk

5 Talk about these points with the others in your class.
- Take it in turns to describe an advertisement which you like. Say why you like it (is it informative, funny, artistic or entertaining, etc?)
- Do you think advertising is a good or a bad thing
  – in newspapers and magazines?
  – on television?
  – on street hoardings?
- What kind of things do you dislike in advertisements?
  What kind of things do you find offensive?
  What sort of advertisements do you like?
- Do you think there should be some kind of control over what is put into advertisements? If so, what would you like to see banned?

Round the World by Concorde

Orlando: 2 nights • Las Vegas: 2 nights • Honolulu: 2 nights
Fiji: 2 nights • Sydney: 2 nights • Bali: 2 nights
Singapore: 2 nights • Delhi: 2 nights • Cairo: 1 night

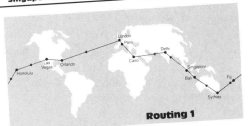

Routing 1

Tour price **£11,950** per person sharing a twin
 £890 single room supplement

Price includes:
– London/Paris/London by scheduled service.
– All flights from Paris back to Paris by Air France Concorde, which is at the disposal of the KUONI party for the complete trip.
– Deluxe and superior first-class hotels.
– Full breakfast daily and a welcome and farewell dinner.
– In-flight meals including drinks and champagne.
– A sightseeing tour in each destination.

Tour highlights
– Colourful, world famous Walt Disney World.
– Sydney's beautiful harbour and Opera House.
– Excitement of oriental Singapore and the casinos of Las Vegas.
– Full day visit to the breathtaking Taj Mahal.
– The Pyramids and Sphinx of Egypt.
– Beautiful beaches of Bali, Fiji and Hawaii.

---

15 days
£1280

Himalayan Trekking

Each trek follows well-established trails and is accompanied by an experienced local guide (Sirdar), sherpas and porters who carry all the equipment, camping gear and food. They will set up each camp and prepare all meals, leaving each individual trekker to walk the trail at his or her own pace. The treks are designed for any reasonably fit person who can manage 5–6 hours walking a day.

ITINERARY
1st day Leave London for Delhi.
2nd day Continue to Kathmandu and stay at the Annapurna Hotel.
3rd day Fly to Pokhara and commence trek to Naundanda. 4 hours walking.
4th day 6 hour trek and overnight at Birethante.
5th day After a 5 hour walk, stay at Tirkhe Dhunga.
6th day 5 hour trek up to Ghorepani (9,000 ft.).
7th day Magnificent sunrise before trekking on to Ghandrung (6 hours).
8th day After 5 hours walking, camp at Dhampus Ridge.
9th day Trek 5 hours and camp on the banks of Phewa Lake.
10th day Walk to airport to catch the flight to Kathmandu.
11th day Excursions to Bhadgaon and Patan.
12th day Fly via Varanasi to Agra. Overnight at the Taj View Hotel.
13th day Visit to Taj Mahal and fly back to Delhi.
14th day At leisure in Delhi at the Taj Palace Hotel.
15th day Fly Delhi to London.

What kind of holiday?

1 a) Read about these holidays.

How many places would you visit on each one?
How much time would you spend in each place?
What do you think you would do in each place?
What are the good points about each holiday?
What are the bad points?
Which holiday would you prefer? Why?

b) Talk to your partner about the holidays and compare your views.

Vocabulary

2 Mark these words SLOW (S) or FAST (F) in the boxes below. Use your dictionary if you need to.

walk ☐ rapid ☐ stroll ☐ wander ☐ fly ☐ amble ☐ swift ☐
quick ☐ gradual ☐ leisurely ☐ run ☐ relaxed ☐ hasty ☐ gentle ☐

Can you think of any more words to add to the list?

Work in groups of four. Compare your words. Add any new words to your list.

3 Look at this list of forms of transport.

☐ train ☐ bus ☐ lorry ☐ bicycle ☐ motorbike ☐ Concorde
☐ car ☐ boat ☐ hovercraft ☐ air balloon ☐ aeroplane ☐ helicopter

a) Which form of transport is the fastest? Which is the slowest? With your partner, put them in order of speed by writing numbers 1–12 in the boxes above (1 = fastest, 12 = slowest).

b) Which form of transport do you like best? Which would you *not* enjoy? Why/Why not?

Talk to your partner. Do you agree? Write down your answers.

	FAVOURITE FORM OF TRANSPORT	WHY?	LEAST FAVOURITE FORM OF TRANSPORT	WHY?
Me				
My partner				

Talk about travel

4 Work in groups of four. Decide which is the best way for you to travel (for example, the fastest, cheapest, most comfortable or most interesting) for the following:
a) from your home to school/college/work
b) from London to Paris
c) from Europe to Australia
d) from the East Coast to the West Coast of America
e) from your home to your favourite place for a holiday
f) around the world

Now imagine the same journeys with:
– your eighty-year-old uncle   – two small children (a baby of
– six heavy suitcases   six months and a two-year-old)
Would you change your mind about the best way to travel?

Fast or slow?

5 People often say that life is getting faster every year. But does faster mean better?

Talk to your partner. Do you think FAST or SLOW is better for each of these things?
COOKING   (What about fast food?)
ART   (Think about painting and photographs.)
COMMUNICATION   (Think about writing letters and telephoning.)
LEARNING A LANGUAGE   (What about intensive language courses?)
GETTING FIT   (Think about crash diets and exercise programmes.)

Class talk

6 Talk about these points with the others in your class.
- Do you think life is faster than when you were young? Is it better?
- Do you think being able to travel to other places more quickly makes life better today?
- Do you think being able to communicate quickly with other people makes life better?

Family Life

Talk about families

1 a) Look at these pictures of different families.

Which size family is the nearest to yours? _____

Which size family would you like to be in now? _____

And in ten years' time? _____

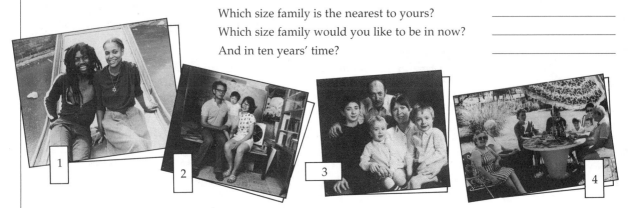

b) What are the advantages and disadvantages of each family size?
Fill in the chart below.

FAMILY	ADVANTAGES	DISADVANTAGES
1		
2		
3		
4		

Now talk to your partner. Find out what he/she has written. Do you agree? Which points do you disagree about?

2 a) Write down all the words you think of when you think of family life. Think of positive words and negative ones!

noise ———— FAMILY LIFE ———— love

b) Work in groups of four. Compare the words you have written down. Have you all thought of similar words? Or are they all very different? How many times did each word appear? Did some words come from everyone in the group? If so, which ones?

Children or not?

3 a) Work in groups of four to six. Write down all the reasons you can think of *for* having children, and then all the reasons *against* having them.

REASONS FOR HAVING CHILDREN	REASONS AGAINST HAVING CHILDREN

b) As a whole class, put together all your reasons *for* and *against* having children. Which list is longer?

What do you think?

4 a) Work in groups of five. Look at these statements, talk to each other, and decide whether you agree or disagree with each one. Write down in the columns how many people in your group agree and disagree with each statement.

	AGREE	DISAGREE
A Work is the most important thing in life.		
B It isn't possible to combine a happy family life with a successful career – for men or women.		
C Everyone should think carefully about having children – some people are not suited to be parents.		
D People should not be allowed to have more than two children.		
E Men and women should share equal responsibility for bringing up children.		
F The state should pay women to stay at home and look after the children.		
G Children are the future of the world, so a parent's job is the most important one.		
H Women are more fortunate than men – they can usually choose whether they work or not, but men are expected to support the family.		
I Family life comes to an end if the mother works.		

A problem to solve

5 Work in groups of three to discuss this problem. What is your solution?

Sarah and Peter Bradley both work. He is marketing manager in a small computer company. She works part-time as a lecturer in a college of education. They have a six-year-old daughter, Alice, who is at school from 9.00 to 3.30 every day. One day, Alice is not very well; she has a temperature and needs to stay in bed. Sarah has to work that morning and asks Peter to stay at home and look after Alice. He refuses, saying he has a busy day, and must go to work. He says that as Sarah works part-time, she should stay at home. Sarah points out that she has just started her job, and that she will lose it if she appears to be unreliable.

What should they do?

Class talk

6 Tell the other groups your solution to the problem above. Listen to their solutions.

- Have any groups thought of the same solution?
- How many different solutions are there?
- Which one is the best?

Telepathy ✓

Vocabulary

1 a) Use the letters given in brackets to complete the words for these objects:

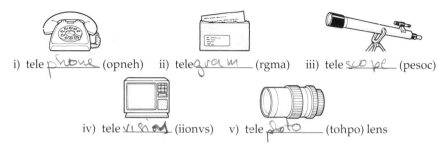

i) tele _phone_ (opneh)   ii) tele_gram_ (rgma)   iii) tele _scope_ (pesoc)

iv) tele _vision_ (iionvs)   v) tele _photo_ (tohpo) lens

b) With all of the objects numbered i) to v), a message is sent and/or received over a distance. Is the message received aurally (through your ears) or visually (through your eyes)?

	i)	ii)	iii)	iv)	v)
aurally	✓				
visually			✓	✓	

c) Here's another word beginning with *tele*:

What do you and the others in your group understand by this word?

Uri Geller

2 Uri Geller is a man who became famous for his demonstrations of telepathy. Some people were (and still are) sceptical about him. This cartoon was drawn after a television programme during which many people found that strange things had happened in their homes. Some people found that old and broken watches had started ticking, others found that their television aerials had bent – all because Uri had concentrated on them.

"IF URI COMES ON AGAIN MISSUS, SWITCH OFF."

Let's try a typical Uri Geller telepathic happening. Find a partner and sit back to back. You both need a paper and pencil. One person should do a very simple drawing and concentrate on it very hard! The other person should concentrate on receiving the message, and try to draw the same simple drawing.

Compare drawings afterwards – are there any similarities at all? If there are any similarities, why do you think they're there? Can you believe that this has got anything to do with telepathy?

Telepathy or coincidence?

3 a) Here is a true story (at least, the person who told it said it was true) about a telepathic happening. The sentences of the story are in the wrong order. Work with your partner to decide on the correct order. When you've finished, read your story aloud to make sure it's in the right order.

4. I didn't have much money and couldn't afford to phone them.

9. There was my boyfriend, in one of the telephone boxes.

7. I wanted to tell them that I was coming home at the weekend.

12. But I hadn't received it – I didn't know he was coming to visit me!

10. 'Hello', he said, 'I was just trying to get through to your school.'

1. Some years ago, I spent six months abroad – at a language school.

5. There wasn't a phone in the place where I was staying, so they couldn't phone me either.

11. He said he was glad I'd received the message the day before, asking me to meet him at the station.

2. In my second week a postal strike started, and it lasted for a long time.

6. One morning I walked to the main station where I wanted to use all the money I had to phone my boyfriend and my parents.

3. I was unhappy because I couldn't write to my family or my boyfriend.

8. When I reached the telephone box, I couldn't believe my eyes.

Now compare your story with that of two other students.

b) Do you think this story has got anything to do with telepathy or was it all just a coincidence?

Make your teacher talk!

4 Ask your teacher
a) if there's another story he/she has heard about a telepathic happening
b) if he/she really believes in telepathy

Class talk

5 Talk about these points with the others in your class.
● What stories have you heard about strange, possibly telepathic, happenings?
● What do you really think about telepathy? Does it interest you? Or do you think it should be left alone?
● Do you know anyone who is telepathic?

Traditional and Modern

Vocabulary

1 a) Which of these words and expressions do you associate with MODERN? Which of them do you associate with TRADITIONAL? Use a dictionary if you want, and put the words into the columns below.

new   antique   old   classic   old-fashioned   new-fangled
obsolete   fresh   avant-garde   fuddy-duddy
archaic   current   novel   up-to-the-minute   antiquated

TRADITIONAL	MODERN

b) Which of the words above are *positive*? Which are *negative*? Put a tick (✔) next to the positive words and a cross (x) next to the negative ones.

Talk to your partner. Do you agree?

Which style do you prefer?

2 Look at these pictures carefully. Take it in turns with your partner to describe each pair of things. Which style do *you* prefer for each thing (traditional or modern)? Do you and your partner both agree?

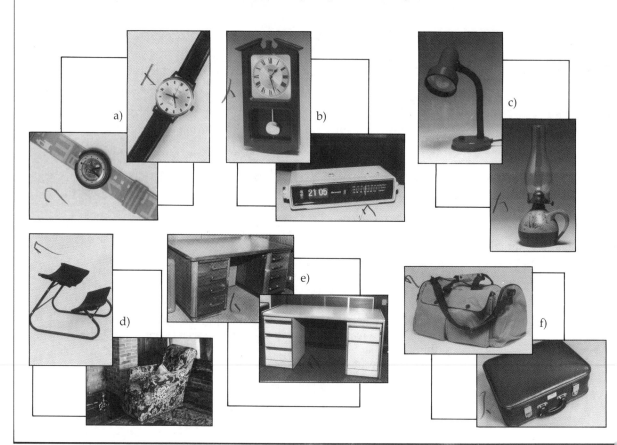

a) b) c) d) e) f)

Rooms and people

3 a) Look at these two rooms. Which one do you prefer? Why?

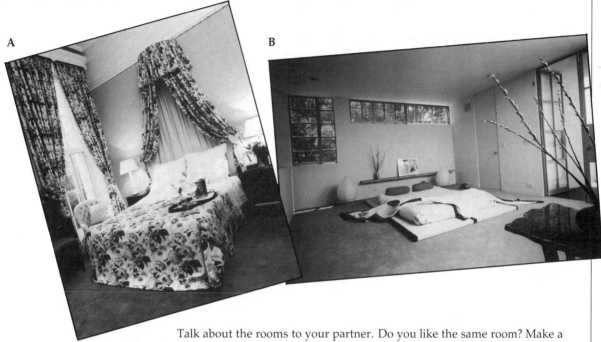

A

B

Talk about the rooms to your partner. Do you like the same room? Make a list of any differences in your opinions of the rooms.

b) Now work in groups of four. Imagine the people who might live in each room.

What kind of people are they?
How old do you think they are?
What jobs do they do?
Have they got any children?
What sort of clothes do they wear?
What is their taste in music?
What about their taste in food?
What does the rest of the house look like?

c) Do you think you can tell what people are like from their homes?
What might people be able to say about you from your home?
Tell each other about yourself. Begin like this:
If you saw my home/room, you'd think . . .

d) Think about your grandparents' home. Can you think of anything from their home which you would love to have in your home? Is there anything you would hate to have?

Class talk

4 Talk about these points with the others in your class.
- How traditional (or modern) are you in your taste?
- What about the class as a whole?
- Has your taste changed as you've got older?
  How do you think it might change in the future?
- What sort of things do you think young people will like in twenty years' time? Do you think you'll like them or not?

UNIT 9 Childhood

Looking back

1 Here is a questionnaire about your childhood. Fill in the answers for yourself, then ask your partner for his/her answers. Talk about the similarities and the differences between you.

	ME	*MY PARTNER*
A What was your position in the family (e.g. only child, oldest, youngest, second of four, etc.)?		
B How did you feel about school?		
C Who was your favourite relative when you were a child?		
D Which toy did you like most?		
E Who did you play with?		
F What did you hate eating?		
G What's your most vivid memory of the house or flat where you grew up?		
H What smells or sounds can you recall from your childhood?		
I What's your earliest memory of your life?		
J Describe your favourite photo from your childhood.		

2 a)

> When I was a child I used to bite my finger nails — my mother tried all sorts of things to make me stop.

> My favourite age was ten because I *loved* my teacher.

> I always wanted to become a train driver, but that wasn't a job for girls, so I used to spend all my time watching the trains go by.

Work in groups of four. Finish these sentences, and then tell the others what you wrote.

When I was a child I used to _____ .

When I was a child I always wanted to _____ .

When I was a child I used to spend my spare time _____ .

My favourite age was ____ because _____ .

b) Tell each other about each of the following.
  i) something you did as a child that you now regret
  ii) something that <u>disappointed</u> you once when you were a child
  iii) an event from your childhood that makes you smile now when you think of it

Helping children

3 These are all organisations that work to help children. Which children do you think they help? Where? What do you think they spend their money on?

¹ RNIB: Royal National Institute for the Blind
² NSPCC: National Society for the Prevention of Cruelty to children

If you had a lot of money and wanted to help children, which children would you try to help (you can choose any group or individual, even one that hasn't been mentioned before here)? Do you ever feel sorry for children? If so, which children?

Class talk

4 If you think your class is too large, make groups of six to eight to do this activity. What can you remember from your childhood? Here's your starter:

HEALTH IN CHILDHOOD

Talk about topics connected with your starter word for ten minutes. One person should make a note of the topics covered. When you've finished tell your teacher and other students in your class about the 'route' your conversation took.

Becoming an Adult

When did you grow up?

1 The *Sunday Times* asked people when they felt they had finally said goodbye to their childhood, and become an adult. Here are some of their answers.

'Manhood finally struck home on the day that I left the Army. It had to do with facing up to the dull, dreary routine of life. Adulthood with its weekly wage-packets and protecting the crease in one's trouser-knees was all that lay ahead.'

Willis Hall, playwright

'I was 15 years old and my brother Tim was 10 when we learnt my father only had weeks to live. We were told there had been a number of heart operations for this sort of complaint but no one over the age of 30 had survived. Nothing was ever going to be the same again.'

Rosie Barnes, Member of Parliament

'Experience has taught me to behave like an adult when it's necessary, which is quite a lot of the time. Therefore I work, pay bills, answer letters from lawyers and accountants, and consider how what I do today will affect tomorrow. But I don't think it's wise to give up childhood so as much as possible I've held onto mine. I'm 41 and 14 concurrently.'

Marsha Hunt, singer

'I have been pretending to be grown up for some 25 years now. I know precisely the moment it happened: lying in hospital, I turned my head to the side to meet a pair of piercing blue, two-minute-old eyes, totally dependent on me. A slow realisation . . . "My God, she thinks I know what I'm doing!" I've been playing Mummies and Daddies ever since.'

Jane Asher, actress

With your partner, read what each person says about growing up. Then talk about what they say, and write down your answers to the questions in the chart below.

	WILLIS HALL	JANE ASHER	MARSHA HUNT	ROSIE BARNES
Does he/she feel grown up?				
When did he/she feel they grew up?				
Do they think it's a good thing to feel?				
What do they say about it?				

Vocabulary

2 a) Write down *three* words you would use to describe the feeling of being grown up.
Write down *three* words you would use to describe the feeling of being young.

b) Now work in groups of four. Put your lists together. Were any of your words the same? Are your words to describe being grown up positive or negative? What about your words to describe being young?

c) Now share all your words with the whole class. Make two lists of the words you all thought of. Which list is more positive?

When can you . . .?

3 Here is a list of 'landmarks' when young people in Britain are allowed to do certain things.

a) With your partner, decide at what age you think young people in Britain are allowed to do these things, and mark your answers in the chart below.

	AGE			
	14	16	17	18
a) leave home with parent's consent		✓		
b) vote				
c) go to prison				
d) leave school and start work				✓
e) get married with parent's consent		✓		
f) leave home				✓
g) drive a car		✓		
h) buy cigarettes				
i) go into a pub, and buy and drink alcohol				✓
j) get married				✓
k) ride a motorbike		✓		
l) go into a pub, but not buy or drink alcohol		✓		

Check your answers in the key on page 63. Were you right?

b) Work in groups of three, and write a similar chart for young people in another country (your own or another one you know well).

Now compare your charts. Which things are the same? Which ones are different? Why do you think they're different? Are children and young people treated differently in some countries?

Class talk

4 a) Think about these questions.

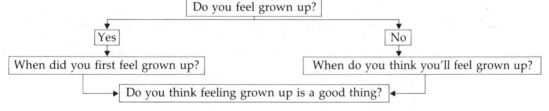

- Talk to your partner, and discuss your answers to these questions.
- Do you feel the same about some things? Talk about the differences you feel, and the reasons for them.

b) Carry out a class survey, to find out how everyone feels.

- How many people in the class feel grown up? How many don't? (Don't forget to ask your teacher!)
- What are the main landmarks people think about when growing up?
- How many people think it is a good thing to feel grown up? How many think it's better to feel young?

Old Age

Talk about people

1 What can you say about the everyday lives these old people lead?

2 a) Fill in the names of people in these boxes.

   i) your oldest living female relative

   ii) your oldest living male relative

   iii) the oldest woman ⎫ (not relatives) who you see from
   iv) the oldest man ⎭ time to time

b) Change books with your partner and find out the following things about these people:

For i) and ii) find out
– who the relative is
– how much contact there is between your partner and this relative

For iii) and iv) find out
– who the person is
– how your partner knows the person
– what your partner's feelings towards the person are

Talk about your feelings

3 Work in groups of three or four. Before you talk to the others write as much as you can about how you would like to be and what you would like to do when you're old. Think about your old age from as many different aspects as possible.

I'd like to . . .

Now compare what you have written with the others in your group. If there are other suggestions that you like too, you can add them to your list (if you agree with them).

Help for old people

4 In Britain, anyone over the age of sixty can have a Senior Citizens Railcard. This allows them to buy train tickets at reduced prices.

a) Describe any special help that people over a certain age in your country get (with travel or anything else).

b) What, in general, are the attitudes towards old people in your country?

They are respected and helped. ☐

They are neglected by a society that prefers the young, the beautiful and the modern. ☐

c) What happens to old people in your country when they can't look after themselves any more?

They are looked after by their families. ☐

They spend their old age in special homes for old people. ☐

If your class has got people from various countries in it, find someone from another country and compare your answers. If you are all from the same country, find out if everyone gave the same answers.

Pros and cons

5 When I'm old I'm going to . . .

> . . . leave this country and go and live somewhere completely different. I don't know where — I'll have to think about that.

> . . . find a voluntary job to do. I'd like to help other people. I've worked all my life — why should I stop?

> . . . travel round the world like a lot of young people do. I want to visit all the interesting countries there are.

Work with a partner and think of some positive points about these plans, and some difficulties these people might meet.

Class talk

6 Talk about these points with the others in your class.
- What differences can you see between what you used to be like in the past and how you are now?
- What changes do you expect to happen in your future?
- What do you think you can look forward to when you retire?
- What might be less pleasant about becoming old?

Dirt and Rubbish

> ## London Airport
>
> Last night in London Airport
> I saw a wooden bin
> labelled UNWANTED LITERATURE
> IS TO BE PLACED HEREIN.
> So I wrote a poem
> and popped it in.

Christopher Logue (b. 1926)

Vocabulary

1 a) Sort out these words into those which mean DIRTY and those which mean CLEAN.

filthy   grubby   spruce   mucky   spotless   spick-and-span
immaculate   grimy   fresh   messy   stained   smart

b) Talk to your partner and compare your answers, then check them in a dictionary.

Talk about your feelings

2 a) Do any of these dirty things upset you? Put them in order, beginning with the one that upsets you most.

a dirty child   3

a dirty fork in a restaurant   7

a dirty car   8

a dirty toilet   1

a dirty kitchen   4

a dirty bathroom   5

a dirty glass in a bar   6

a dirty food shop   2

b) Work in groups of four to six. Compare your lists. Do the same things upset you all? Or different things?
Think of other dirty things which you don't like.

3 What is your attitude to dirt and rubbish?

Think about each of the following statements and rate your attitude to each one on the scale 1–10 (1 = strongly disagree, 10 = strongly agree).

	MY SCORE	MY PARTNER'S SCORE
A My bedroom is always very tidy.		
B There are more important things to worry about than cleanliness.		
C I think people who throw litter on the streets should be fined or put in prison.		
D An untidy home is a home full of busy and happy people.		
E It's impossible to keep a large city clean.		
F Other people's untidiness doesn't bother me at home.		
G People should not be allowed to wash their cars on Sundays.		
H You can't expect children to be clean and tidy.		
I A tidy desk is the sign of an organised mind.		
J It's a full-time job to keep a house clean and tidy.		

Now talk to your partner, and compare your scores.

Talk about your attitudes to dirt and rubbish. Does your attitude to tidiness change depending on what you are thinking about (for example, a kitchen, your study, someone else's house, a city street, and so on)?

Using rubbish

4 It often seems a pity to throw out a lot of rubbish, when some of it could be reused.

a) In groups of three, think of ideas for using these things instead of throwing them away. Write down as many as you can!

a plastic carrier bag

a pile of old newspapers

a pair of old socks

an old food can

a glass wine bottle

an old saucepan

a plastic litre bottle

a cardboard box

b) Share your ideas with the rest of the class. How many ideas have you thought of for using each thing? Which is the most useful thing? Which is the least useful?

c) Have you got any other ideas for using things which might be thrown away?

Class talk

5 Of course, some people's rubbish is other people's treasure!

- Can you think of anything your parents threw out which you would like?
- Is there anything you've thrown out which you wish you hadn't?
- Do you think your children will wish you hadn't thrown some things out?
- What things which we now treat as rubbish do you think might be valuable one day?

Vocabulary

1 a) Most people are afraid of something! If that fear is extreme – for example, if a person is so afraid of flying that they just can't travel by air – then that fear could be called a phobia.

What are the people here afraid of? Find the words here.

h__ghts   sn**a**k**e**s   l**u**fts   mo**u**s**e**   st**o**rms   the d**a**rk

Missing letters:
a a e e e i i i o

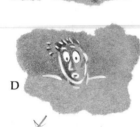

A She's afraid of _____

B He's afraid of _____

C He's afraid of _____

D He's afraid of _____

E He's afraid of _____

F They're afraid of _____

b) How afraid of these six things are you? Write the letters of the pictures next to the best comment for you in the table below. Then ask a partner and fill in his/her letters. Ask your teacher, too.

	YOU	YOUR PARTNER	YOUR TEACHER
I'm not at all afraid of			
I'm a little bit afraid of			
I'm rather afraid of			
I'm very afraid of			

c) Work with a partner and decide what it is that makes these people afraid of these things.
Example:
Perhaps the girl who is afraid of mice thinks they are dirty animals and carry disease.
Perhaps she's afraid of them because they run so fast. Maybe she thinks they could bite her. The thought of a mouse running up her leg might be awful for her.

2 Work in groups of five or six. Fill in the last word of these sentences, and then tell the others in your group about the things you are or used to be afraid of.

I am When I was a child I used to be	not very fond of _____. a bit scared of _____. afraid of frightened of } _____. terrified of _____.

Tell the group about other people you know or knew, using these sentences.

Explaining phobias

3 a) This is what happened to a small boy many years ago:

That small boy is now a man, but he is still very afraid of storms. Can you understand why?

Work with your partner to invent explanations about what possibly happened to these people when they were children.
  i) A woman who is afraid of big black dogs.
  ii) A man who is afraid of going to see the dentist.
  iii) A woman who is afraid of going under water when she's swimming.
  iv) A man who is afraid of being in a room with the door closed.

Now make a group of four with two other students and compare your explanations.

  b) Stay in your group of four. Tell the others about a moment in your past when you felt afraid.

Class talk

4 What do you think people could be afraid of when they think about the future? They may be afraid of getting old, for example, or of losing their jobs. They may be afraid of something that might happen in the world or to them personally. Do you feel just a little bit afraid of anything when you think about the near or distant future?

UNIT 14 | Women and Men

Talk about people

1 a) These statements were made by children. Find four endings for the boy and four for the girl from this list.
   i) then I'd be able to wear trousers more often.
   ii) then it would be all right if I cried.
   iii) then a _____ would ask me for a date.
   iv) then I could play football.
   v) then I could have long hair.
   vi) then I wouldn't have to help with the washing up.
   vii) then I wouldn't have to carry all the heavy things.
   viii) then I'd be able to help dad repair the car.

I'd like to be a girl because . . .   I'd like to be a boy because . . .

b) Use the ideas in the statements above to make a list of things usually expected of girls and those most often expected of boys. Do this with a partner, and then add two more usual expectations for the girls and two for the boys.

A questionnaire

2 a) Fill in this questionnaire by yourself.

	♀	♂
What sex are you?		
If you grew up with both parents, which one did you feel closest to?		
What was your favourite toy when you were a child?		
What was your favourite subject at school?		
What subject did you dislike most at school?		
What was your hobby when you were a child?		
What did you expect of your future when you were a teenager?		

b) Compare your answers   i) with someone of the same sex.
                          ii) with someone of the opposite sex.
c) Collect the answers from everyone in your class on the board, in two categories – *male* and *female* answers. What similarities and differences are there?

Have a guess!

3 Here are some statistics about people in America. What do you think the answers to these questions are? You probably don't know the answers for sure, but have a guess!
a) Who live longer – men or women?
b) Are there more men or women in America?
c) Which group has the highest percentage of unemployment – men or women?
d) Who are there more of – male prisoners or female prisoners?
e) Who marry younger – men or women?
f) Which group has the highest percentage of smokers – men or women?
g) Who is more likely to die of heart or related diseases – men or women?
h) Who is more likely to die of cancer – men or women?
When you've made your decisions, compare with a partner. Then look at page 63 where you can find some statistics about these points.

Talk about your feelings

4 Work in groups of three or four. Which of these things could you:
a) accept completely?
b) find unusual but acceptable?
c) find unusual and a bit strange?
d) not be able to accept?

	a)	b)	c)	d)
a woman as a political leader				
a woman as a pilot				
a woman as a miner				
a woman as an active soldier				
a woman as a religious leader				
a man as a beautician				
a man as a children's nurse				
a man as a secretary				

Can any of you remember ever being surprised to find a man or a woman doing a particular job, or having a particular function?

Class talk

5 Share your opinions about being male or female. Talk about:
• yourself in relation to society's image of your sex – what is that image?
• yourself in relation to advertisers' image of your sex – do you fit in?
• what you think must be the best things and the worst things about bei[ng] member of the other sex in your country.

Strange Stories

Fact or fiction?

1 a) Read these stories, and decide whether *you* think they're true or false. Mark your answers in the boxes below each story.

The tallest person in the world was Robert Pershing Wadlow, who died in 1940. He was 8'11" or 272 cm tall.

	ME	MY PARTNER
True False		

The shortest person in the world was a Dutch woman, Pauline Musters. She was only 20" (51 cm) tall.

	ME	MY PARTNER
True False		

In America, a family had four children with birthdays on the same day. Catherine was born in 1952, Carol in 1953, Charles in 1956 and Claudia in 1961 – all on 20th February!

	ME	MY PARTNER
True False		

A Russian woman is reported to have had sixty-nine children between 1725 and 1765. They included sixteen twins, seven triplets and four sets of quadruplets.

	ME	MY PARTNER
True False		

The oldest reported person in the world was Shigechiyo Izumi from Japan, who was born on 29th June 1865. He lived until he was 118 years old.

	ME	MY PARTNER
True False		

The worst sneezing fit known is that of Donna Griffiths of Britain. She sneezed from 13th January 1981 to 15th September 1983. She stopped on 16th September – the 978th day!

	ME	MY PARTNER
True False		

b) Talk to your partner, and find out whether you agree. Mark your partner's answers in the boxes. If you disagree, what differences were there between you?

c) Talk to your teacher. Find out whether each story is true or false. Were you right?

Do you believe in ghosts?

2 a) This story was told by an English actor, Jon Pertwee. Each section tells part of the story, but the sections are all in the wrong order. With your partner, put them in the right order to find out what happened.

A He used to come in up the stairs, look at us, then go through to the next room to make sure that Michael was all right, and then he used to go back downstairs and out of the back door. We loved it when he did this; it made us feel loved and wanted.

B I slept upstairs with my stepbrother in one room, and my brother Michael used to sleep in the other. There was a door between the two rooms.

C We three boys knew that when we were on our own we had all heard someone come up the stairs into our bedrooms, then go downstairs again and out of the back door. Yet father said he had never been near the house. Of course, there was no electricity then, and it was completely dark at night. So we never saw anyone, and we never found out who it was.

D This story happened to my two brothers and me. Many years ago, we were staying in a little cottage in Devon. It had two rooms upstairs and two downstairs.

E Once, when we knew he was going out to dinner miles away, we said, 'There's no need to come back to the house this time, Dad, we'll be perfectly all right.' 'What are you talking about?' he asked. 'Why *should* I come back?' We said, 'Well, you usually do.' We were very surprised when he said, 'Whatever do you mean? I've never, ever come back, when I've left you boys alone.'

F When father went out in the evening, he used to say, 'Will you boys be all right?' We said, 'Of course, we're fine.' But we were always very relieved when we heard father come back to make sure we were all right.

When you have finished, check your answers in the key on page 63 to see if you've put the story in the right order.

b) What do you think really happened? Discuss the story with your partner, and then tell the rest of the class what you think. Do you all agree? How many different solutions to the story have you all thought of?

Tell a story

3 In groups of four, think of a strange story. It can be one you've heard, or read about, or you can invent one of your own. Take it in turns to tell your stories. Be prepared to think of solutions to all the stories! Who told the best one?

Class talk

4 Talk about these points with the others in your class.
- Do you like ghost stories?
- Do you believe in ghosts?
- How would you feel if you thought you saw or heard a ghost?
- Would you ever stay in a house which people said was haunted?

UNIT 16　Animals

Talk about your feelings

1

Look at these pictures.

Where are the dogs?
Why are they there?
What are they doing?
What do you think of each picture?

b) Talk to your partner about the pictures. Do you feel the same about them?
Do you disagree about anything?

2 a) In your country, which of these animals would you
i) eat?
ii) keep as a pet?
iii) treat as a wild animal?
iv) use as a working animal?

Fill in your answers below.

ANIMAL	EAT	KEEP AS PET	TREAT AS WILD	USE AS A WORKING ANIMAL
cat				
dog				
horse				
deer				
rabbit				
squirrel				
fox				
duck				
goat				
camel				
frog				
mouse				

b) Now work in groups of four. Find out what everyone's answers are, and add them to the chart. Tell the others about your answers.

Now compare your answers. Which animals do you agree about? Which ones do you disagree over?

Pros and cons

3 a) Now read this article.

Pupils Watch Pets Killed

Horrified pupils at the George Land School in Hertfordshire have seen their favourite farm animals killed and sold for meat.

Parents are worried that their children will be permanently upset by this.

One mother said that her 13-year-old daughter had been looking after rabbits at the school farm, and had been shocked to find three of them dead. 'I think it's terrible,' she said. 'My daughter was extremely upset when she came home from school.'

Another mother said that many parents were opposed to the killing, but were frightened to say anything in case their children were expelled from the school.

But the headmistress, Mrs. Jill Johnson, defended the farm. She said it was one of several in the area, and that it is supported by local veterinary surgeons. 'Where town and country meet, there is bound to be a clash of views on life,' she added. 'But it's an approved policy in rural schools, and only the children who want to take part in the scheme do so. They're not forced to.' She agreed that some children become very fond of the animals and are upset when they are killed. However, she hoped those children would speak out and start a discussion about it. 'The school has an active animal rights group, and many of the girls are vegetarian,' she added.

Children are told when the animals are to be killed, and can choose whether to watch or not. Children who want to skin the animals can do so. The larger animals are sent to a slaughterhouse, and sold as meat.

One mother spoke in favour of the scheme. Mrs Janette Salter said her 13-year-old daughter, Dominique, had a responsible attitude towards animals as a result of working on the farm. 'She has no fear, and if she had to she could kill her own pet rabbit,' she said.

b) When you have finished reading the article, decide whether you agree or disagree with what the school is doing. Form two groups: those who agree with the school and those who disagree with it.

Make a list of all the points in the article which support your view. Add any more points you can think of.

Now make a list of all the points for the opposite point of view. Add any more points you can think of.

Form small groups of six to eight. Discuss the points you have thought of, for and against what the school is doing. What do *you* think?

Class talk

4 Talk about these points with the others in your class
- People often say that in Britain, animals are treated better than children. Is this true in your country?
- Do you think animals are a substitute for children for some people?
- How do you think animals should be treated? Do you think some people make too much fuss of them?
- Do you think we should eat them? Use their fur? Keep them as pets? Take care of them? Use them for work? Put them in zoos? Let them go free?

UNIT 17   Festivals and Holidays

Talk about holidays

1 a) Make a list of some of the festivals and holidays in your country.
   b) Compare your list with your neighbour's. Are they similar? Which ones are different?
   c) Tell the rest of the class about your list.
      Make a class list of all the festivals and holidays you have thought of. If you know of any special holidays in other countries, add them to the list.
   d) Look at your list again. Which of the festivals and holidays are religious? Which ones are related to the different seasons of the year? Are any of them national days?
   e) Each person should choose one festival or holiday. Work singly or in small groups, and prepare a short talk to explain what the holiday is, and how people celebrate it. Tell the rest of the class about your festival or holiday.

2 Of course, not all special days are holidays. Here are some days which are special in Britain. Some are holidays, and some are not.

February 14th
April 1st
May 1st
October 31st
November 5th
December 26th
December 31st

   a) Work in groups of four or five (if possible, mixed nationality groups). Discuss each date. What is it called? Is it a holiday? What do people do then? Is it a special day in *your* country?
   b) Tell the rest of the class what you have found out! If there are any dates which you're not sure about, ask your teacher.

Vocabulary

3

SUMMER HOLIDAY

   a) How many words can you find in these two words? You may use each letter in the words once in each new word. So you can have MUM because there are two 'M's, but you can't have DAD because there's only one 'D'. Work with a partner, and write down as many words as you can!
   b) Share the words you've found with the rest of your class. How many did you find between you? Who found the most?

Are holidays a good or bad thing?

4 a) Read this article about people going on holiday. Which things are people worried about? Which things do they like about holidays?

We're just too worried to have fun on holiday

Most people in Britain take their troubles with them on holiday, according to a new survey.

40% said the most important reason for going away is to escape stress, but almost everyone said they worry more than they do at home. Only 4% are happy and carefree.

The most common concern is burglary: 4 out of 10 people worry about their homes being broken into while they're abroad.

More than a quarter are afraid they'll be upset by noisy holiday makers, and 22% are worried about being mugged.

One in five think the car may break down, and the same number are upset about the chances of bad weather.

One in seven people said their idea of a good holiday is 'sun, sea and sex'. A quarter of all young, single men thought this was the best formula for a holiday, according to the MORI[1] survey.

The research showed that the traditional stay-at-home Briton is no more. Three out of every five adults now want to holiday abroad. Three years ago, less than half wanted to go overseas.

The hotel holiday is still the most popular. Just over half the people interviewed preferred being looked after to going on a self-catering holiday, despite worries about cheeky waiters and noisy fellow guests!

[1]*MORI:* Market and Opinion Research International

b) Work in groups of four to six. Make a list of all the good points and bad points about going on holiday. Add your own ideas.

Tell the rest of the class about your list. Put all your points together. Which list is longer?

Class talk

5 Imagine you can go on holiday for a month. You can go wherever you like and spend as much money as you want. What kind of holiday would you choose? Write down your ideal holiday.

Now, tell the rest of the class.
- Did any people choose the same kind of holiday as you?
- Has anyone thought of something you'd like to do?
- Which is the most popular holiday?

Pet Hates

Vocabulary

1 a) Look at these expressions. Find three which mean to hate something, three which mean to not like something, and three which mean to feel neutral about something. Write them in the boxes below.

I'm not keen on it.   I can't stand it.
I detest it.   I don't like it.
It doesn't worry me.   I don't mind it.
I loathe it.   It doesn't bother me.
I dislike it.

FEEL NEUTRAL	*NOT LIKE*	*HATE*

b) Talk to your neighbour. Are your answers the same? Check your answers with the rest of the class.

Talk about your feelings   2

‘I hate people who chew gum and talk at the same time.'

‘I can't stand dogs' mess on pavements.'

‘I loathe finding hairs in my food.'

‘I hate people who tread on your toes and then say "Sorry".'

‘I hate fried eggs.'

‘I really dislike shop assistants who ignore you.'

Look at the pet hates at the bottom of page 44.
a) What is your pet hate? Why? Write it here.
   My pet hate is _____ because _____ .
b) Ask your partner, and write the answer here.

   My partner's pet hate is _____ because

   _____ .
c) Now tell the rest of the class about your partner's pet hate. Have many people chosen the same things? Which is the most popular pet hate?

3 a) Of course, you can have pet hates about all sorts of different things. Fill in this chart with all yours.

PET HATES	YOU	YOUR PARTNER
Food		
Animals		
Clothes		
At work		
At home		
Irritating Habits		

b) When you have finished filling in the chart with your pet hates, talk to your partner and fill in the second column. Do you share any pet hates? Which ones are similar? Which are very different?
c) Now report back to the rest of the class. Tell them what you have found out. Listen to the other reports.

Were any of the pet hates a surprise?
What were the things people hated most?

A problem to solve

4 What can you do about pet hates? Some of them are very reasonable, and some are totally irrational. Is there a cure to stop you hating something?
a) In a group of three, choose six pet hates, and decide how you would try to stop them.
b) Tell the rest of the class about your 'cures'. Which ideas were the best? Which were the silliest? Would any of them make the pet hate worse?

Class talk

5 Talk about these points with the others in your class.
• Are pet hates permanent? Is there anything you used to hate, which you don't mind now? Or even positively like? Is there anything you used to love, but now hate?
• Do you think pet hates change as you get older? Do you have more? Or fewer? The same? Or different?
• Do you think most people become more or less tolerant as they get older?

Hot and Cold

Vocabulary

1 Decide which of these words are 'hot' words and which are 'cold' words. There are eight of each.

to bake   to boil   to burn   chilly   cool   a fan   a fire   to freeze
a fridge   frost   ice   to melt   to scald   to shiver   to sweat   warm

HOT	COLD

Find a solution

2 Talk to your partner and decide on the best solution to these problems. Look at the example to help you.

Example:
If the weather were too hot for me, I'd eat ice-cream all day.

a) What would you do if the following things were too hot for you?
the weather
the bath water
your food at a rather formal dinner
your seat next to a window on a train
a casserole you want to take out of
    the oven
your tea or coffee

b) What would you do if the following things were too cold for you?
the weather
your soup in a restaurant
the room you're in now
your bed
the water in the shower in your
    friend's house where you're staying
    for a weekend
your home

Make a group of four with another pair of students. Find out their solutions by asking questions for each problem.

Example:
What would you do if the weather were too hot for you?

Vocabulary

3 Look at the pictures below. They are all things that people sometimes have to make the temperature hotter or colder.

Work with someone who comes from a country with a similar climate to yours. Divide the things shown above into the following categories:

REALLY NECESSARY	HELPFUL	NOT NECESSARY

A change of climate

4 If the climate were much hotter than it is or much colder than it is, what differences do you think there would be in your country?

Examples:
If our climate were much hotter, people would probably have a sleep after lunch.
If our climate were much colder, people would probably all have central heating.

Think of three suggestions for *hotter* and *colder*, and then compare your suggestions with those that someone else has made.

Make your teacher talk!

5 You can add more questions to each of these. Find out:
a) if he/she has ever been to a very hot country
b) if he/she has ever been to a very cold country
c) if he/she likes the climate of the place where he/she lives
d) if the weather is important to him/her

Now *you* talk about the four points above with a small group of other students.

Class talk

6 If your class is large, make groups of six or eight to do this. Here's your starter word:

FIRE

Talk about topics connected with your starter word for ten minutes. One person should make a note of the topics covered. When you've finished, tell your teacher and other students in your class about the route that your conversation took.

Addiction

Talk about people

1 a) Look at these photos.

A

B

C

Work in groups of three or four, and discuss the following questions in relation to the three people in the photos above.
  i) How far is what the person is doing generally acceptable?
  ii) What are the possible negative effects this person's habit could have on other people?
  iii) How does what the person's doing have a negative effect on himself/herself?
  iv) What is the attitude of the law towards this person and his or her habit?

b) What differences can you see between a drinking habit and a drug habit? Think of some possible answers to these questions. Do this by yourself.

	THE ALCOHOLIC	THE DRUG ADDICT
When do you think the person had his/her first experience with alcohol or drugs?		
Where do you think this first experience took place?		
Who else do you think was also involved in this first experience?		
How easy is it to buy alcohol or drugs?		
How easy is it to become addicted?		
Why is giving up so difficult?		

Now tell a partner what you've written. Compare and discuss your answers together.

2 a) Read this article about an organisation which tries to help people to give up.

Helping addicts keep a balance

by Jeannine Williamson

PEOPLE with drink and drug problems have a new opportunity to ask for help.

The Libra Trust has opened a base in Eastbourne staffed by full time co-ordinator Keith Rowley and a team of volunteers.

For the last 14 years Libra has held group meetings in the town in rooms "borrowed" from other groups.

Now the charity has its new base in Vincents Yard off Susans Road.

Keith, 46, and his helpers will be on hand five mornings a week to meet and help people.

Keith, who gave up his job as a furniture polisher to work at the centre said: "I first got in touch with Libra ten years ago when I had an alcohol problem. I started drinking when I was in the army and found it helped me get over my insecurity and then I found it had got out of hand and I was an alcoholic.

"I had been to other groups but I liked Libra's informal atmosphere and friendly approach and I now want to help others in the same position."

Each week between 12 and 20 people attend the group meetings in Eastbourne. Keith said: "We have all sorts of age groups coming here. I have met a 14-year-old girl who has an alcohol problem; a 16-year-old boy on heroin and people over 60 with problems."

Libra co-founder Ric Evans, who lives in Lewes, said: "Alcohol is a bigger problem than all the drugs put together.

"But having said that we are not against alcohol. Some people find the only way they can get over their problem is to give it up while others can control and limit it. We are here to help people improve their lives."

Work with a partner to plan a short radio interview about this organisation. One of you is the radio interviewer, the other is Keith Rowley. You have a maximum of three minutes' radio time, so choose your questions carefully and plan the answers in detail.

b) Here's a letter that was received by the organisation *LIBRA*. Work in groups of three or four, and make a list of points of advice you would give the writer.

Useful expressions for giving advice:

It may help you to . . .
If I were you I'd . . .
Well, one solution may be to . . .
In your situation I think I'd . . .
It might be a good idea to . . .

Dear Mr Rowley,
   I need some help badly. My husband, who lost his job last year and has been unemployed ever since, has become an alcoholic. Don't get me wrong - he used to drink before he lost his job, but now it has really become a problem. We often used to go out for a drink in the evening together, but we never had more than one or two - and it was always a pleasure. Now he just sits around all day, feels useless (so he says) and starts drinking even before lunch. I find that I'm beginning to drink more, too. This is not just to keep him company, but I've developed the idea that if I drink it, he can't. Before I just used to nag him but that didn't work. What can we do now? Can you help us? I'm sure our two children, aged eleven and eight, will soon begin to suffer - if they haven't already.
                                    Mrs D. M. (Eastbourne)

Class talk

3 When we think about addiction we nearly always think first of smoking, alcohol and drugs.
 - What do you think might be the problems of a person who:
    – can't stop working?
    – can't stop eating?
    – can't stop gambling?
 - What do you think could be the consequences of these habits for the person concerned and for others?
 - If you have ever known anyone who was or is addicted to any of the things mentioned in this unit tell the rest of your class something about that person.

UNIT 21   Noises and Sounds

Talk about sounds

1 a) What sort of noises or sounds would you expect to hear if you were

in the country?	in a reference library?
walking along a busy	in a prison?
shopping street?	on a beach in a holiday resort?
in a dentist's waiting room?	in a churchyard?

Which of these noises or sounds are pleasant to hear, and which are unpleasant?

Work with your partner to decide on a noise or sound that would be most unexpected in each of the above places.

b) Close your eyes for one minute (your teacher will tell you when to open them again). When the minute is over, the class should collect together a list of all the sounds and noises heard during that time. So concentrate hard on what you can hear.

Have a try!

2 Here is a tongue twister about noise. Say it five times, as fast as you can, with a partner. One of you should ask the question, the other should answer.

WHAT NOISE ANNOYS AN OYSTER MOST?
A NOISY NOISE ANNOYS AN OYSTER MOST.

Attitudes towards noise

3 Look at these two comments about noise.

'I do not like noise unless I make it myself.' (a French proverb)
'A noisy man is always in the right.' (William Cowper, 1731–1800, a poet)

What do these comments say about people's attitudes towards noise? How much truth can you see in them?

Remembering sounds

4 Work with a partner. Describe seven short situations in which you or other people heard these noises or sounds. What made the sounds? Why were they welcome, frightening, nostalgic, etc.?

a welcome sound	an irritating sound
a frightening sound	a threatening noise
a nostalgic sound	a chilling sound
a deafening noise	

Make a group of four with two others, and tell each other the situations or stories you have thought of.

A problem to solve

5 What would you do in these situations? Make your decisions first, then discuss them in groups of four or five. There's room at the end for you to add your own solution if you've got a better one.

a) You're in a hotel room. You wanted to have a peaceful, relaxing couple of days. It's eleven o'clock in the evening, and the person in the room next to you has got the television on very loud. What do you do?

☐ phone the person in the next room and complain

☐ bang on the wall

☐ phone reception and complain

☐ turn your television on, louder than the one in the next room

☐ put ear plugs in your ears, get under the bedclothes and try to ignore the noise

☐ _____

b) You're in a train on a long distance journey. The person in the seat next to you is listening to pop music on a Walkman. It's much too loud and you can hear it very well. What do you do?

☐ go to the restaurant car for a long lunch, although you aren't hungry

☐ ask your neighbour to turn the volume down

☐ glare at your neighbour very angrily

☐ move to a different compartment

☐ give up trying to read and look out of the window instead

☐ _____

c) You're having lunch with an old friend in a very nice hotel restaurant. You've got years to catch up on, and your friend is soon going to live abroad. When you booked the table, they didn't tell you that there was a jazz band playing at lunchtime. It's impossible to hold a conversation. What do you do?

☐ leave after the first course and refuse to pay the bill

☐ ask for your lunch to be served in one of the hotel rooms

☐ buy all the musicians lots of drinks so that they have to take a very long break to drink them

☐ shout at your friend so loudly that you disturb everyone else

☐ give up and listen to the music

☐ _____

What experiences have you had of noises like these?

Class talk

6 Talk about these points with the others in your class.
• Where do you think this notice was seen?

> PLEASE THINK OF OTHERS!!
>
> Noise after 10 pm disturbs many people. Please be as quiet as you can. Thank you.

• Where else can you see notices about noise? Do you think a notice like this makes any difference? Would it make any difference to you?

• Tell the others about yourself – are you a noisy person? Do you ever like being noisy? Do you ever make a noise (like typing or running up and down the stairs) that you know could annoy someone else? Are you very sensitive to noise? Which noises disturb you most?

UNIT 22 | Work

Different working styles

1 Different countries have different styles of working. So, for example, Japanese companies are very different from those in Europe.

a) Do you think these statements are more likely to be made about Japanese or European companies?

    i) People expect to work for the same company all their lives.

    ii) People wear different clothes, according to their job and position in the company.

    iii) There is a company song which everyone sings.

    iv) Everyone wears the same clothes.

    v) People expect to change jobs and companies during their working lives.

    vi) The directors eat in the canteen with the workers.

    vii) There is often a big difference in salary between the directors and the workers.

    viii) Everyone in the company does physical exercises together during the working day.

    ix) The size of an office often indicates the position of the person in it.

    x) Employees are expected to put the company's interests first.

    xi) There are different places for directors and workers to eat.

    xii) In some companies there is a 'hire and fire' attitude to workers (that is, they take on employees when needed, and dismiss them for little reason when they are no longer needed).

b) Compare your answers with the rest of the class. Do you all agree?

Do you think these differences in working style reflect the differences between the societies?

Talk about work

2 a) In groups of three, write down six things you would tell a visitor to your country about working life there. For example, should visiting business people expect to use first names or surnames when talking to others? How many hours should they expect to work each week?

b) Tell the rest of the class about your list. Which ideas are the same? Which are different? What difficulties would there be for a British or American person coming to work in your country?

Vocabulary

3 a) Write down all the words you can think of related to the word WORK. Think of both positive and negative things!

routine ——— WORK ——— salary

b) Now work in groups of six to eight. Compare your words. How many words have you got the same? How many are different? Are there any words which you've all written down? Are there any words which only one person has thought of? Do your words reflect the way you think about work?

How much is a job worth?

4 Jobs are valued differently in different societies. Jobs which are highly paid in some countries are badly paid in others. Those which have a high prestige in some countries have low prestige in other places. A teacher in Britain, for example, has relatively low pay and low prestige. This can be marked on a pay/ prestige chart as follows:

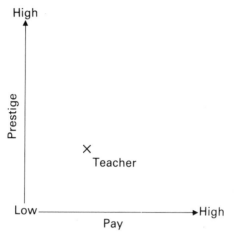

a) Mark on the chart where a teacher's position in your country would be.
   Now mark in where you would put each of these in your country:
   a waiter   a nurse   an actress   a secretary   a police officer
b) Compare notes with your partner.
c) Now work in groups of four to six. Choose six more jobs, and place them on the chart.
d) Tell the rest of the class which jobs you chose, and where you have put them.

What can you say about how different jobs are valued by society? Are difficult or dangerous jobs paid more? Are jobs which require no training paid less? How do you think jobs should be valued?

Class talk

5 Talk about these points with the others in your class.
- What kind of job do you do or would you like to do?
- How is that job valued in your country?
- Do you think it is over-valued or under-valued?
- What are the general attitudes to work in your country? Do you agree with them?

Optimism and Pessimism

The two extremes

"I DON'T THINK I'll LIKE IT."

1 a) What does the picture on the left tell you about the pessimist? Have you ever behaved like this ostrich?

b) Work with a partner. One of you should think about an optimist who sees the positive side of everything, and the other should think about a pessimist who sees everything negatively. Answer these questions from the optimist's and the pessimist's point of view.

	OPTIMIST	PESSIMIST
What's your favourite colour?		
Which is your favourite month?		
Which is your favourite season?		
What sort of films do you like watching?		
Which foreign language do you like hearing?		
What are you going to do when you retire?		
What did you read in the newspaper yesterday?		

c) Make a group of four with two others and compare the answers you've given.

What would they say?

2 a) Work in pairs. What do you think the optimist and the pessimist would say about these things?

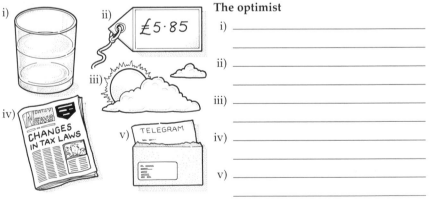

The optimist

i) _____

ii) _____

iii) _____

iv) _____

v) _____

The pessimist

i) _____

ii) _____

iii) _____

iv) _____

v) _____

b) Compare your suggestions with two other students.

3 a) In this cartoon, Augusta's two friends seem to be rather pessimistic about her holiday:

What is it they fear about the water, the food and the air?

b) What negative points do you think a pessimist would express to:
  i) a friend who has found a house to buy?
  ii) a friend who has just had an interview for a new job in a new, rather small computer company?
  iii) a friend who has bought a very cheap charter ticket for a very long flight with a completely unknown charter company?

A quiz

4 Are you an optimist or a pessimist? Do this quiz and find out!

1. If you had just started a new job and immediately found that you didn't like it, would you
  a) leave after one day?
  b) leave after a week?
  c) stay longer to see if things improved?

2. If you ask someone to give you some help, do you
  a) know they will agree?
  b) think they may agree?
  c) feel sure they will disagree?

3. When you get post in the morning, do you expect it to contain
  a) good news?
  b) bad news?
  c) nothing of interest to you?

4. If a relative contacts you after years of silence, do you think they
  a) want something from you?
  b) have realised they've missed you?
  c) want to tell you that someone in the family has died?

5. If your boss suddenly called you into his office one Friday afternoon, would you think
  a) he was going to offer you a better job?
  b) he was going to tell you to leave?
  c) he wanted to talk about something very routine?

6. If you went for an interview for a job and didn't get it, would you assume that they
  a) found someone better than you?
  b) realized you were too good for the job?
  c) just didn't like you as a person?

7. A good-looking member of the opposite sex is watching you from the other side of a crowded room at a party, do you
  a) think you must look attractive, too?
  b) feel that there must be something wrong with your clothes?
  c) tell the friend you're with that the stranger is looking at him/her?

Ask your partner to turn to page 64 and help you to assess how optimistic you are.

Class talk

5 Talk about these points with the others in your class.
  • What things (such as birds singing, for example) make you feel optimistic?
  • What things make you feel pessimistic?
  • What do you sometimes do to cheer yourself up if you're feeling down?

UNIT 24   Anger

Vocabulary

1 a) In this word search game, you will find eight words which all mean 'angry'. The words go downwards or across. ANGRY has already been done for you. Work with your partner. How many more can you find?

F	U	R	I	O	U	S	W	A
L	D	C	R	O	S	S	I	N
I	X	M	A	D	P	R	L	N
V	P	N	T	R	W	X	D	O
I	Y	T	E	A	N	G	R	Y
D	X	V	W	Y	B	M	P	E
I	R	R	I	T	A	T	E	D

b) Which three words mean 'not very angry'?

_____

_____

_____

Which two words are colloquial ways of saying 'angry'?

_____

_____

Proverbs

2 In groups of four to six, look at these proverbs. Decide what you think they mean. Do you agree with what they say? Why/Why not?
a) When people are angry, they cannot be in the right. (Chinese proverb)
b) A hungry person is an angry person.
c) Anger is a short madness.
d) People who get angry slowly stay angry longer.
e) Let not the sun go down upon your anger. (Ephesians 4:26)
f) When angry, count to a hundred.

Talk about your feelings

3 a) What makes you angry? How do you show your anger? Think about your feelings, and then write your answers in the chart below.

	YOU	YOUR PARTNER
What makes you angry? How do you show your anger?		

b) Now talk to your partner. Ask them the same questions, and fill in the chart.
c) Talk to the rest of the class. Tell them about your partner. Listen to all the answers.
d) What makes people angry most often?
   How do most people show their anger?

What would you do?

4 a) Now work in groups of three. Look at these situations. How would you behave in each situation? Would you get angry? How would you show your anger? Or would you try to control yourself?
   i) A visitor to your home accidentally breaks your favourite vase.
   ii) Your child runs across the road without looking at the traffic, and nearly gets run over.

iii) Someone pushes in front of you in a queue in a busy shop.
iv) Someone bumps into your car when you are waiting at the traffic lights.
v) Your favourite television programme is cancelled because a sports programme goes on too long.
vi) A friend telephones to say they can't come and see you tonight as planned, because they've been invited to a party.
vii) Your husband/wife/girlfriend/boyfriend forgets your birthday.
viii) Someone leans out of their car and makes a rude sign at you, shouting that you're a bad driver. You don't think you've done anything wrong.
ix) In the park, someone's dog jumps up at you, and covers your coat in mud.
x) In a restaurant, the waiter ignores you and begins to serve other tables although you were sitting there first.

b) Now talk to the rest of the class. Did they feel the same way as you? Or did they react differently? How did most people react to each situation?

5 How do you react when people are angry with you? Do you get angry back? Apologise? Burst into tears? Walk away?
a) Talk to your partner. Compare your reactions. Do you react in the same way? Or differently?
b) Find out from other people in the class how they feel. What did you find?
c) How do most people react to anger?
Do men/women react differently?
Do younger/older people react differently?

A problem to solve

6 Here is a letter taken from the Problem Page of a magazine.
a) In groups of four to six, read the letter, and decide what advice you would give.

> *Dear Aunt Clare,*
>
> I have a very strange problem – I'm married to a man who never gets angry. At first I thought it was wonderful to be with such a gentle person, but nothing ever makes him cross, and it's beginning to upset me. We can never have a proper argument, because he doesn't like arguments. He just shrugs his shoulders and leaves the room if I shout at him. Why do you think he's like this? What can I do to change him?
>
> Mary S.

b) Tell the other groups what your advice would be to Mary S.

Have any groups thought of similar advice? Which piece of advice do you think is the best?

Class talk

7 Talk about these points with the others in your class.
● Is anger a good emotion? Is it better to be angry and express your feelings? Or is it better to try to stay calm and hide your feelings?
● Do you get angry easily? Or rarely?
● Do you try to stay calm or do you show your anger?
● Have you ever been angry and regretted it? Or not been angry and regretted it afterwards?

Crime and Punishment

Vocabulary

1 Match the words with the definitions given below.

☐ drug smuggling ☐ shoplifting ☐ fraud

☐ arson ☐ kidnapping ☐ hijacking

☐ pickpocketing ☐ mugging ☐ theft

a) they broke the window of his car and stole the radio
b) they sold paintings that they knew weren't genuine masterpieces
c) they illegally carried drugs into another country
d) they held a pistol at the pilot's head and he had to do what they said
e) they set fire to the hotel
f) they took some things off the shelves and left the supermarket without paying for them
g) they took away the rich man's son and asked him for a lot of money
h) they hit the man on the head as he was walking along the street, and stole all his money and credit cards
i) they took her purse out of her handbag as she was standing on the crowded platform waiting for the train

Talk about punishments

2 a) Which of these punishments exist in your country? Discuss this with a group of other people who, if there are various nationalities in your class, come from different countries.

a fine   a suspended prison sentence   a prison sentence   execution

b) Do you know of any other punishments? For what crimes might someone get these punishments?

A problem to solve

3 Make the punishment fit the crime: A case of murder
At the age of forty-two, Kurt Hofmann, a German businessman, was given a very high position in a large company in Zurich, Switzerland. He took the job as head of the marketing department even though he had not had direct experience in this type of work before. He was very ambitious and really wanted this well-paid job. The company gave him the job even though they knew it was a 'problem' position.

After about six months it was clear that Mr Hofmann was under a lot of stress. Work with a partner and number these stress factors 1–10, starting with 1 as the most serious.

☐ his job was beyond him, he just couldn't do it

☐ his colleagues, five men in particular, disliked him and told everyone how bad he was at his job

☐ his superior didn't help him at all

☐ his wife left him

☐ his girlfriend refused to move to Zurich

☐ he had to move away from the town where he had always lived

☐ he was living in a foreign country

☐ he worked at least twelve hours a day trying to do the job

☐ there was no one at work he could trust

☐ he was living alone for the first time in his life

One day this STOP PRESS report was in the evening newspaper:

He was arrested a couple of weeks later in a hotel a few hundred miles away. When his trial took place months later, lots of comments were made about him.

"I'm a handwriting analyst. Samples of his handwriting over the years show definite signs of instability."

"I work at RAZ. He should be put in prison for the rest of his life – every day of it."

"Mr Hofmann lived in the flat upstairs. He seemed such a nice man. I can't understand it at all. I feel very sorry for him."

"I'm a psychiatrist. I've examined Mr Hofmann and I can definitely say that he is unable to cope with stress. He is not a leader and probably never was."

The consequences of that fateful day were:
- for Mr Hofmann – seventeen years in prison
- for his immediate superior – early retirement with a good pension
- for four employees – death, leaving three widows and seven orphans
- for one employee – unable to work for the rest of his life

Work in groups of four to decide:
a) if you think seventeen years was a fair sentence.
b) if you think any other people were also partly responsible for what Mr Hofmann did.

Give reasons for your decisions.

Class talk

4 What do you think will be the consequences of Mr Hofmann's long stay in prison?

UNIT 26 | Taking Risks

Talk about people

1 a) Look at these pictures. What risks are the people in them taking?

b) What could be the consequences for each of these people if something went wrong in these situations? Would those consequences be of importance to anyone else apart from the person shown?

c) What do you think each of these people could or should do to avoid, or at least reduce, the risk they're taking?

Taking risks

2 a) How willing to take risks are you? Work in groups of four and answer these questions for each person using the following number scale:

5 = yes, I would/3 = maybe I would/1 = no, I definitely wouldn't

Write the names of the four people in your group at the top of the columns below.

NAME				
Would you make a parachute jump?				
Would you fly as a passenger in a two-seater plane?				
Would you go to a country where there is a war going on?				
Would you buy shares without expert advice?				
Would you take a job in a medical centre doing research into highly infectious diseases?				
Would you buy a house near a nuclear power station?				
Would you give up your job without having a new one?				
Would you take part in a seance?				
Would you hold a snake in your bare hands?				
Would you change money on the black market in a country with strict currency regulations?				

b) Now add up all the numbers that you've got on your grid.
Total for my group: ☐
Compare your total with other groups to find out which group in your class is most willing to take risks.

c) Every person in the class should now choose one of the questions he/she answered negatively, and explain what the risk is that they wouldn't be willing to take.

d) Who do you think might take out insurance against the following things? In what circumstances would you expect the insurance company to pay out?

damage to contents of house	death
health problems	adverse weather
cancellation	loss of income
theft	injury to a particular part of
accident	the body (e.g. hands)

What insurance have you got? Is there any insurance that you haven't got, but think perhaps you should have?

3 a) Work in groups of four or five. Agree on lists of the three most serious risks the following people might take:
i) a Hollywood stunt man
ii) an air hostess
iii) a policeman
iv) a tourist going to a very primitive country with little knowledge of local customs and no knowledge of the language spoken there

b) Now compare your lists with other groups' and collect all the suggestions made in one class list.

Risks – your responsibility?

4 a) Here is the warning that is printed on cigarette packets in Britain:

GOVERNMENT WARNING
Smoking can seriously damage your health.

How far do you think the government should be responsible for our willingness to take risks? Do you think the government should:

	YES	NO
i) print warnings like this on cigarette packets?		
ii) make it compulsory to wear seat belts in a car?		
iii) introduce compulsory AIDS tests for all people?		
iv) allow no alcohol at all for drivers?		

b) Compare your yes/no decisions with others in your class and discuss your opinions briefly.

Class talk

5 What do you think is the greatest risk you can take:
- with your health?
- with your money?
- with a friendship?
- with a possession which means a lot to you, but isn't valuable?

Tell the others in your class about risks you have taken, whether you knew it or not at the time.

Answer key

UNIT 3

4 'Touch wood!'
In Britain, if someone is talking about something they hope will happen or continue, they often say 'Touch wood!' afterwards. So, a friend might say, 'My new job is going well – touch wood!' This means that they hope the good luck will continue, and won't change just because they have talked about it. The person saying it often touches something made of wood as they speak. The expression dates back to when people believed that good spirits lived in trees, and touching a tree preserved the good luck.

UNIT 4

1 The advertisement is for Sheraton Hotels.
2 Advertisement A is for Spa Supermarkets (caption: SPAR. SO NEAR, SO GOOD.)
Advertisement B is for K shoes (caption: LEATHER MEETS THE FRENCH POLISHER.)

UNIT 7

1 a) i) telephone   ii) telegram   iii) telescope
iv) television   v) telephoto lens
3 Correct numbering: 4, 9, 7, 12, 10, 1, 5, 11, 2, 6, 3, 8

UNIT 8

1 **traditional:** antique, old, classic, old-fashioned, obsolete, fuddy-duddy, archaic, antiquated
modern: new, new-fangled, fresh, avant-garde, current, novel, up-to-the-minute

UNIT 10

3 The landmarks for young people in Britain are:
14 years: go into a pub, but not buy or drink alcohol
16 years: leave school and go to work
16 years: leave home with parent's consent
16 years: get married with parent's consent
16 years: buy cigarettes
16 years: ride a motorbike
17 years: drive a car
17 years: go to prison
18 years: leave home
18 years: get married
18 years: go into a pub, and buy and drink alcohol
18 years: vote

UNIT 13

1 a) A – mice   B – lifts   C – heights   D – the dark
E – snakes   F – storms

UNIT 14

3 a) women (75.5 years, men 67.9)
  b) women (51.2% of population, men 48.8%)
  c) women (9.3% of female labour force, men 7.6% of male labour force)
  d) men (92.9%, women 7.1% of prison population)
  e) women (20.7 years, men 23.4 years)
  f) men (41% smoke, 34% of women smoke)
  g) women (56%, 51% of male deaths)
  h) women (19.3%, 18.6% of male deaths)

UNIT 15

1 ● Tallest person in the world – true.
  ● Shortest person in the world – false. Pauline Musters was 23.2" (59 cm) tall.
  ● Most children – true.
  ● Coincident birthdays – false. The Cummins family actually had *five* children with the same birthday! Cecilia was born in 1966. Random odds against five siblings having the same birthdate are one in 17,797,577,730!
  ● Oldest person – false. Shigechiyo Izumi died on 21st February 1986. He lived to 120 years and 237 days.
  ● Worst sneezing fit – true. It is estimated that Donna must have sneezed about a million times in the first 365 days!
All these facts are from the *Guinness Book of Records 1988*.
2 The original order of the story is: D, B, F, A, E, C

UNIT 17

2 **February 14th:** St Valentine's Day
Traditionally the day when people send a card or present to their sweethearts (girlfriend or boyfriend). St Valentine is the patron saint of people in love.

April 1st: April Fools' Day or All Fools' Day
The day when people play practical jokes on each other. These may be quite simple jokes, or more complicated ones such as the amusing (but false) stories printed by some national newspapers.

May 1st: May Day
Traditionally a day when people celebrate the beginning of spring with dancing and songs. It is also celebrated as a day for the workers. It has been an official public holiday since 1978.

October 31st: Hallowe'en
The eve of All Saints' Day (November 1st). A popular day with young people who celebrate it by dressing up in witches' and ghosts' costumes and playing games.

November 5th: Guy Fawkes' Night
Another popular celebration with young people, when bonfires are lit and fireworks are set off, both in public parks and in private gardens. Historically, it is to celebrate the fact that Guy Fawkes failed to burn down the Houses of Parliament in 1606.

December 26th: Boxing Day
The day after Christmas Day is a public holiday. In the past, it was the day when people gave 'boxes' (money or presents) to the people who worked for them.

December 31st: New Year's Eve
The last day of the year, when parties and dances are held to celebrate the arrival of the new year. In Scotland, Hogmanay, as it is called, is a big celebration. In many large towns, people gather in a public place to see the new year arrive together. The following day, January 1st, is a public holiday.

UNIT 23

4 Scores:
1. a: 0 b: 5 c:10
2. a:10 b: 5 c: 0
3. a:10 b: 0 c: 5
4. a: 5 b:10 c: 0
5. a:10 b: 0 c: 5
6. a: 5 b:10 c: 0
7. a:10 b: 0 c: 5

Results:
65–70 You really are a great optimist!
55–60 You are quite an optimist, but not always.
45–50 You are half optimist, half pessimist.
35–40 You are rather a pessimist, try to look on the brighter side.
Under 35 Oh dear!

UNIT 24

Words across: furious, cross, mad, irritated
Words down: livid, irate, wild, annoyed
not very angry: cross, irritated, annoyed
angry (colloquial): mad, wild

UNIT 25

1 a) theft b) fraud c) drug smuggling
d) hijacking e) arson f) shoplifting
g) kidnapping h) mugging i) pickpocketing